THUCYDIDES ON POLICY, STRATEGY, AND WAR TERMINATION

Karl Walling

Even the ultimate outcome is not always to be regarded as final. The defeated state often considers the outcome merely as a transitory evil, for which a remedy may still be found in political conditions at a later date.

CLAUSEWITZ

War is like unto fire; those who will not put aside weapons are themselves consumed by them.

LI CHUAN

For decades, Thucydides's account of the Peloponnesian War has been a staple of professional military education at American war colleges, the Naval War College especially.[1] And with good reason—he self-consciously supplies his readers a microcosm of all war. With extraordinary drama and scrupulous attention to detail he addresses the fundamental and recurring problems of strategy at all times and places. These include the origins of war, the clashing political objectives of belligerents, the strategies they choose to achieve them, and the likely character of their conflicts. As the war escalates, Thucydides expands his readers' field of vision. He compels them to consider the unintended consequences of decisions of statesmen and commanders and the asymmetric struggle between Athenian sea and Spartan land power. He shows the ways in which each side reassessed and adapted to the other; the problems of coalition warfare; indirect strategies through proxy wars, insurgencies, and other forms of rebellion; the influence of domestic politics on strategy, and vice

Professor Walling served as an interrogator in the U.S. Army, 1976–80. After earning a BA in the liberal arts from St. John's College in Annapolis, Maryland, in 1984, he was awarded a joint PhD in social thought and political science from the University of Chicago (1992). He has been a research fellow at the Program on Constitutional Government at Harvard University and the Liberty Fund. He has been a professor of strategy at the Naval War College, first in Newport, Rhode Island, and currently in Monterey, California, from 2000 to the present. His publications include Republican Empire: Alexander Hamilton on War and Free Government *and (together with Bradford Lee)* Strategic Logic and Political Rationality.

© 2013 by Karl Walling
Naval War College Review, Autumn 2013, Vol. 66, No. 4

versa; and myriad other enduring strategic problems that those who wage war at any time ignore at their peril. As a student of war and politics, whatever his faults, he was a giant with few peers, if any at all. Yet Thucydides says relatively little about peace, peacemakers, and peacemaking. Not surprisingly, then, what he has to say on this subject often receives little attention at the war colleges, especially when there are so many other rich questions to explore in his account.

One thing Thucydides does say, however, needs to be pondered carefully to understand the problem of terminating the Peloponnesian War or any other. The Peace of Nicias—at the end of the so-called Archidamean War, a full decade into the twenty-seven-year war between the Athenian-led Delian League and the Spartan-led Peloponnesian League—cannot, he argues, "rationally be considered a state of peace," despite the efforts of peacemakers like Nicias to turn it into one. Instead, it was a "treacherous armistice" or an unstable truce (5.26).[2] Although Thucydides never defines "peace," his distinction between peace and a truce indicates that he had some idea of what peace might mean in theory, even if it was difficult, indeed impossible, to establish it between the Athenians and their rivals in the Peloponnesian League. Peace for him appears to be something very Clausewitzian: the acceptance by the belligerents that the result of their last war is final, not something to be revised through violent means when conditions change or opportunity is ripe.[3]

The Peace of Nicias was not the only occasion when Thucydides treated a peace treaty as a mere truce *(spondē)*. He also used the word "truce" to describe the Thirty Year Peace, the treaty that officially, at least, put an end to the First Peloponnesian War of 462/1–445 BCE (1.115). Some modern scholars, skeptical that the Second Peloponnesian War (431–404 BCE, popularly referred to as simply "the Peloponnesian War") was inevitable, have argued that this agreement was a genuine peace. According to this view, Athens accepted the result of the first war as final and became a "sated power," no longer aiming to expand its empire by force.[4] Thucydides emphatically did not think this was the case, however. Because Thucydides's account of the war is not the same as the war itself, it is possible that Thucydides was wrong, but we will never understand his work unless we try to understand him on his own terms, which is the objective of this article. Indeed, without a serious effort to understand Thucydides's own view of the relation among policy, strategy, and war termination, efforts to analyze his account critically are likely to produce more heat than light. They may even so distort understanding of Thucydides and the Peloponnesian War that they rob both the author and his chosen case study of the enduring strategic value they deserve.

To understand why Thucydides did not think either the Thirty Year Peace or the Peace of Nicias brought the Peloponnesian War to an end, one must pay careful attention to his presentation of the objectives and strategies of the belligerents. The war waxed and waned, and waxed and waned, like a fever (or a plague, Thucydides might say) because of a clash of policies that made it impossible for either Athens or Sparta to accept the result of their most recent conflict as final. Their political objectives were fundamentally incompatible. Athens was determined to expand; Sparta was no less determined to contain Athens, if necessary, by overthrowing its empire and its democratic regime. If so, the Second Peloponnesian War was inevitable, and not because it was predetermined but because the First Peloponnesian War never really ended—that is, neither side was willing to change its revisionist objectives. Each side's objectives clashed inherently with the other's sense of the requirements of its own safety. Each sought to exploit opportunities to revise the settlements of their previous conflicts as soon as opportunity arose. Each placed such high value on its objectives that it would risk war rather than give them up. So the First Peloponnesian War dragged on and on, and then the Second Peloponnesian War, on and on through the Peace of Nicias and beyond, until one side was able to overthrow the other's regime and replace it with something fundamentally less threatening.

The repeated failures to terminate the war, in Thucydides's account, cast the motives, policies, and strategies of the belligerents in a fundamentally different light than typically seen among strategists today. It is common to suggest that Athens under Pericles chose a Delbrueckian strategy of exhausting Sparta and that Sparta, under Archidamus, chose an equally Delbrueckian strategy of annihilating the Athenian army in a major land battle early in the war.[5] If one assumes Athens was a sated power, then there is some sense in describing its strategy as an effort to win, by not losing, a war of exhaustion with Sparta that would maintain the status quo ante. If one follows Thucydides and assumes that Athens was an expansionist power, however, a more ambitious diplomatic and military strategy was going to be necessary, and such a strategy is readily apparent for those willing and able to connect the dots.

Under Pericles especially, that strategy was to break up the Peloponnesian League as a prelude to further expansion in the west, toward Italy and Sicily in particular. Spartan authorities—presuming they understood that the Athenians were attempting to destroy the Peloponnesian League—had little choice but to counter by supporting Sparta's own allies. When Sparta's annual invasions of Attica are seen as part of a larger coalition strategy, they do not look like utopian efforts to achieve a knockout blow, though the Spartans would have been grateful had the Athenians been foolish enough to cooperate by risking a decisive engagement outside their walls. Because Athens' long walls (that is, those reaching about six miles, with a road between, to the port of Piraeus) had rendered it invulnerable to direct assault by the Spartan army, there is good reason to think that Archidamus, especially, understood that Sparta could not win a war of annihilation, that its best option was a war of exhaustion. The Spartans needed to coordinate with actual and potential allies, especially Persia and rebels from the Delian League, to tie down Athens in a multitheater war. So even if the Spartans' annual invasions failed to induce the Athenians to commit strategic suicide by fighting outside the walls or to inflict so much damage on the countryside that the Athenians sued for peace, they contributed mightily to a multitheater strategy of attrition that would force the Athenians to fight everywhere, leaving them strong nowhere. Ultimately that is how Sparta won the war, despite much Spartan incompetence and with much unintended help from the Athenians, who would have achieved a much better outcome if they had been willing to make a genuine peace earlier in the twenty-seven-year war.

So long as the mutually exclusive political objectives of Athens and Sparta remained unchanged, the Second Peloponnesian War was inevitable and unlikely to end. But war as such is not inevitable. One significant inference from Thucydides's account of the failure of the belligerents to terminate this war effectively is that the art of peace is to prevent the violent clash of policies that produce and protract warfare. Although Thucydides makes clear that he does not think Athens was ever a sated power, it should have been. To whatever extent our own world resembles that of Thucydides, he helps us ponder, among many other things, one of the fundamental global strategic problems of the twenty-first century: that both old and new powers will need to find the self-restraint to prevent dissatisfaction with previous peace settlements, which are often mere truces, from escalating into general war.

I

Thucydides had a thesis—that the events and debates immediately before the outbreak of the Second Peloponnesian War were not as important to its origins as something more fundamental, the growth of Athenian power and the fear it inspired in Sparta. Athenian growth and Spartan fear of it constituted the "truest cause" of the war (1.23, 1.88).[6] His *Pentecontaetia*, or history of the fifty years between the end of the Persian Wars and the crises over Corcyra and Potidaea at the outbreak of the Second Peloponnesian War, was designed to prove that thesis. One can summarize his complex argument the following way.

First, despite strategic cooperation during the Persian Wars, Sparta and Athens were deeply suspicious of each other almost from the moment they forced the Persians to retreat from the Greek mainland after the battles of Salamis, Plataea, and Mycale in 480–79 BCE. When Athens began to rebuild its walls in 479, Sparta and its allies, seeing the enormous growth of Athenian naval power during the Persian Wars, began to be afraid. So they made one of the first calls for universal and unilateral arms control, even partial disarmament, in recorded

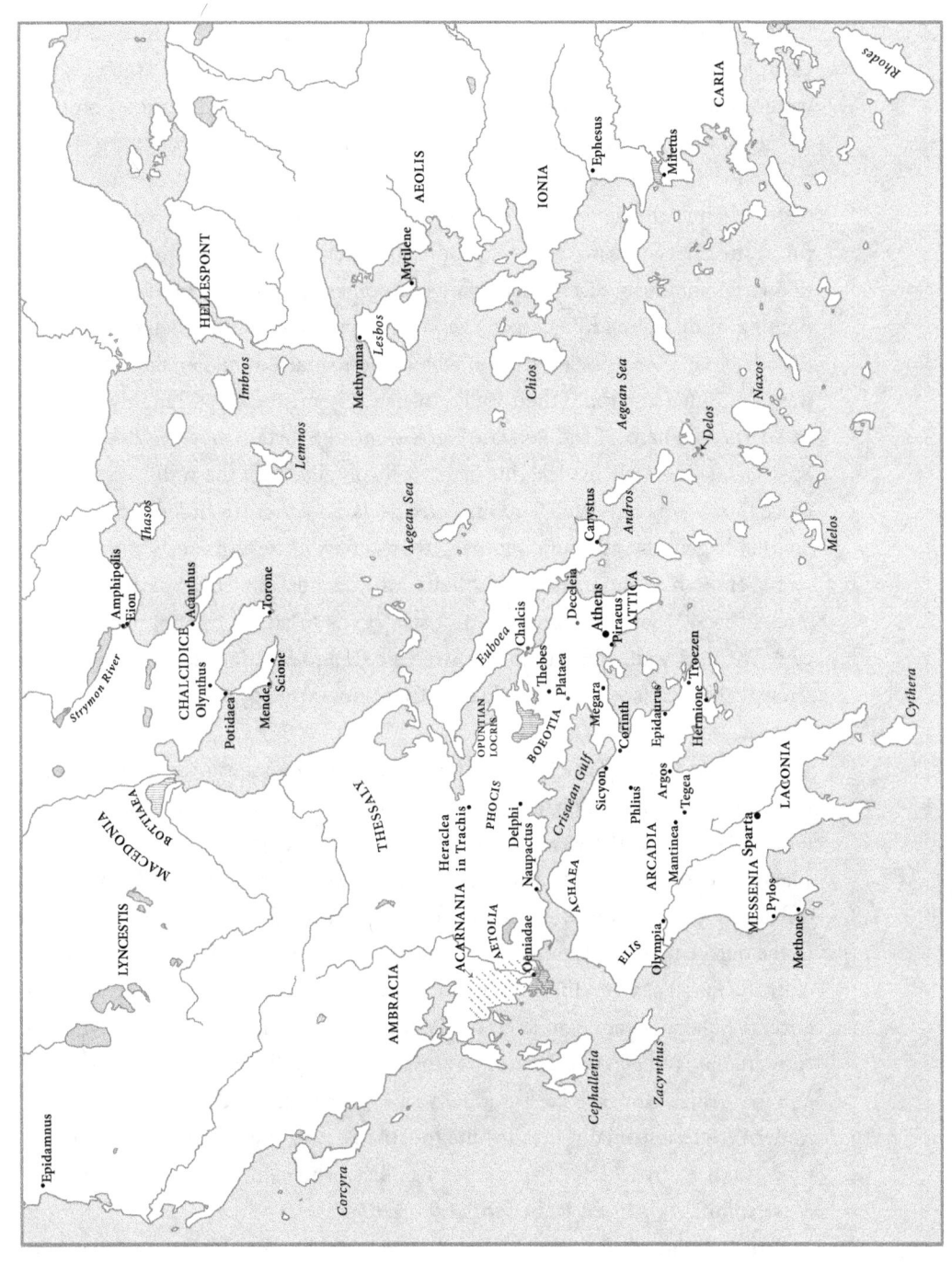

history. They asked the Athenians not to rebuild their walls but instead to join them in tearing down the walls of all the cities in Greece. They argued, disingenuously, that walled cities would merely give the Persians strong points for defense if they invaded again and that anyway all Greeks could retreat to Spartan protection in the Peloponnesus if the Persians returned (1.90). Distrust breeds distrust. The Athenians could not help finding something one-sided and deceitful in the Spartan arms-control proposal, which would leave them vulnerable to Sparta's famously disciplined army of hoplites (that is, armored foot soldiers fighting in disciplined phalanxes) reinforced by forces from its allies. So under the advice of Themistocles, the fox who had outsmarted the Persians at Salamis, they continued to rebuild their walls covertly. Themistocles, still highly regarded in Sparta as a hero of the Persian Wars, went to Sparta, where he deceived the Spartans deliberately by delaying arms-control talks until the walls were rebuilt. Once they were completed Themistocles declared Athenian independence from Spartan hegemony, announcing that Athens knew its best interests and was now strong enough to pursue them without asking permission from Sparta or anyone else (1.91–92). Says Sun Tzu, the best strategy is to attack the opponent's strategy.[7] The long walls, the Athenian "Strategic Defense Initiative," were a breakout strategy that rendered obsolete Sparta's traditional strategy of dominating Greece in decisive land battles.

Second, it was not Pericles, then, but Themistocles who was the father of Athenian grand strategy, which had two components. One was defense by land behind long walls down to Piraeus, the port of Athens, walls that made Athens a de facto island, able to feed itself by sea and invulnerable to attack by land. The other was offense by sea, which the Athenians undertook with the utmost vigor from 479 to the outbreak of the First Peloponnesian War in 462/1. Their objective was to clear the Persians from the Aegean and to build and expand their maritime alliance, the Delian League, to keep the Persians out. It was Themistocles who told the Athenians to become a naval power and thereby "lay the foundations of the empire." Allies-cum-subjects gradually saw their dues for defense transformed, under Pericles especially, into tribute to Athens, thus financing the growing and powerful navy by which Athens ruled its allies, who came to see the city as a tyrant exploiting them for its benefit (1.93, 1.96–99).

Third, seeing all this unfold, Sparta was not idle, though it proceeded cautiously and covertly. When rebels from the Athenian empire on the island of Thasos asked for Sparta's aid in 466/62 (?), the Spartan authorities promised secretly to go to war with Athens, thus establishing a fundamental principle of Spartan strategy (1.101).[8] The best time for Sparta to go to war with Athens was when Athens was already committed to fighting in some other theater. The Athenian walls made it possible for Athens to withstand a siege indefinitely, yet that did not mean Sparta had no counter. If the Athenians were compelled to fight not merely in Attica but also throughout their empire, they might lose the will to carry on or even the empire that enabled them to carry on. In the former case, there could be a negotiated settlement; in the latter, the Spartans just might be able to overthrow not merely the empire but even the democratic regime (arguably the source of all their troubles) in Athens itself.

Timing is often everything, however. Before the Spartans were able to go to war to support Thasos and potentially many other rebel cities against Athens, there was an earthquake in Sparta in 462/1 (?). It enabled the Helots, the enslaved descendants of the Messenians whom the Spartans had conquered previously, and who constituted the overwhelming majority of Sparta's population, to rebel. Rather than fight a two-front war against Athens and the Helots, the Spartans canceled or postponed their plan to attack Athens and instead called on that city, their formal ally, known for expertise in siege warfare, to help them put down the Helots in their last redoubts at Mount Ithome. Traditional Spartan xenophobia, combined with suspicion of the "revolutionary and enterprising" character of the Athenians, led to a change of heart, however (1.102). The Spartans dismissed the Athenians, saying they no longer needed their aid. It must have been about this time that the Athenians learned the Spartans had planned to attack them to support the revolt at Thasos—an important reason for the Spartans to wish them to depart, lest the Athenians betray them first by an alliance with the Helots. Not surprisingly, in light of both Sparta's betrayal and its rejection of their aid against the Helots, the Athenians left Sparta in a huff, broke off their alliance with Sparta, and allied instead with Argos, Sparta's traditional competitor for hegemony in the Peloponnesus, as well as with the Thessalians in the north (1.102).

Fourth, the Athenians allied with Megara, on the Isthmus of Corinth, and actually helped it build its long walls down to the sea, so that it could be resupplied in case of assault (1.103). In effect, in doing so the Athenians extended their own long walls from Attica to the isthmus, with extraordinarily important strategic consequences. Attica would be safe from invasion by land from the Peloponnesus. Sparta would be cut off from its major ally on land—Thebes, in Boeotia. Also, through Megara's port on the Crisaean Gulf, Pegae, Athens had now established a base for expansion in the west. Through the alliance with Megara, which was at war with Corinth, the traditional hegemon in the Crisaean Gulf, Athens engendered bitter hatred on the part of Corinth, a maritime power in its own right and fabled for wealth derived from trade over its isthmus.

Fifth, the Athenians were expanding in all directions in the First Peloponnesian War. In the west, they had control of both of Megara's ports, Nisaea and Pegae. They had already established a base for Helot refugees from Sparta at Naupactus, which could serve as a base for the Athenian fleet in the Crisaean

Gulf (1.103). They gained control of Achaea on the opposite side of the gulf, thus potentially acquiring the ability to bottle up Corinth in the gulf. Toward the south, they acquired Troezen in the Peloponnesus as an ally, presumably as a base for linking up with Argos, if and when Athenians and Argos intended to unite to fight the Spartans in the Peloponnesus. To the north, they sought to extend their hegemony into Boeotia (1.108). Most amazing of all, to the south they gave up on an expedition to Cyprus and decided instead to send two hundred ships to aid a rebellion in Egypt against the Persian empire, presumably to gain access to the grain and the seemingly infinite wealth of Egypt (1.104).

Sixth, the Athenians failed to achieve their objectives in the First Peloponnesian War in large part because they were overextended and fighting in too many theaters. The Egyptians drained the canals of the Nile, thus trapping and annihilating the Athenian naval expedition. In an ironic anticipation of later Athenian failure in Sicily, the Egyptians also destroyed another Athenian fleet sent to reinforce the first (1.109–10). The Boeotians were able to defeat Athens on land at Coronea and so to recover their independence (1.113). The cities of Euboea, from which Athens received much of its food, revolted, thus forcing Athens to divert forces to subdue them (1.114). Most importantly, Megara defected to the Peloponnesian League, meaning the gate to Peloponnesian invasion of Attica was open (1.114).

Seventh, with the entire empire at risk and the Athenians fighting on multiple fronts, Athens had little choice but to agree to the Thirty Year Peace treaty with Sparta and its allies, who demanded a heavy price. The Athenians had to give up Nisaea and Pegae, as well as Achaea and Troezen (1.115). Three of these sacrifices served primarily the interests of Corinth, which could not have wished to confront Athens in the Crisaean Gulf. (Not coincidentally, they were to loom large in Athenian demands during peace talks with Sparta after the Athenians' stunning victories at Pylos and Sphacteria in the Second Peloponnesian War [4.21].) Most importantly, the Thirty Year Peace required Sparta and Athens not to encroach on each other's allies and to settle future quarrels through arbitration.

Largely because Athens had overextended itself, a blunder Pericles refused to let the Athenians forget (1.144), the Spartans and their allies had contained, even rolled back, Athenian expansion, with future controversies to be solved through arbitration, not war. But for how long? The treaty, like most others in Thucydides's account, had an expiration date, thirty years—that is, long enough for both sides to recover from the war, if they were patient. That most such treaties in Thucydides's account come with expiration dates is important. It reveals that most of the treaties not only were but were assumed by the belligerents themselves to be nothing but truces, meaning that the belligerents did not expect final results to their wars. As Herodotus observes, in peace sons bury their fathers, in war fathers bury their sons.[9] Sons cannot replace their fathers, but fathers can have more sons. If they or their children or both do not accept the result of a previous conflict as final, they need only wait until their respective sons reach the age to fight alongside their fathers, brothers, and other kin in the next round of conflict. Hence, in the sentence immediately after describing the terms of the Thirty Year Peace, Thucydides calls it a "truce" (1.115).

Like the Peace of Nicias, it merely bought time for each side to renew the conflict under more auspicious circumstances. Indeed, within six years of signing the treaty a key ally of Athens, Samos, rebelled, compelling Athens, led by Pericles, to engage in a long, costly, and brutal siege to recover it. Significantly, the Peloponnesian League was divided over whether to use this opportunity to force Athens into a two-front war, with Sparta probably supporting going to war at that time but Corinth dissenting. As the Corinthians later reminded the Athenians, were it not for their dissent the Second Peloponnesian War might well have started over Samos in 441 rather than over Corcyra, Potidaea, and Megara in 431 (1.41).[10] So the Athenians knew there was a high probability that any time a significant ally rebelled or was instigated to rebel by the Peloponnesians, Athens would have another multitheater war on its hands.

In other words, "It ain't over 'til it's over," and in ancient Greece, war was never over. One might well debate whether Thucydides's greatest translator, Thomas Hobbes, was right to say that the natural state of mankind is a state of war. One might even debate whether he was right to conclude that international relations, there being no opportunity to exit the state of nature, are by definition a state of war too. But he was certainly right about the ancient Greeks: their natural and normal state was war, not peace,

> for Warre, consisteth not in Battel onely, or the act of fighting, but in a tract of time, wherein the Will to contend in Battell is sufficiently known: and the notion of *Time,* is to be considered in the nature of Warre; as in the nature of Weather. For as the nature of Foule weather, lyeth not in a shower or two of rain; but an inclination thereto of many dayes together: So the nature of War, consisteth not in actual fighting; but in the known disposition thereto, during all the time there is no assurance to the contrary. All other time is PEACE.[11]

The final component of Thucydides's argument that the truest cause of the war was Sparta's fear of the growing power of Athens is rooted in efforts by Athens, Corinth, and ultimately Sparta itself to continue the First Peloponnesian War by indirect means and proxies. One proxy was Corcyra, an island off the northwestern coast of Greece in the Ionian Sea, the other Potidaea, a city on the Chalcidic Peninsula, in the Aegean Sea in northeastern Greece. Corinth was at the center of both controversies. Epidamnus, a colony of Corcyra on the Adriatic, underwent one of the revolutions common in ancient Greece, with the popular party exiling the oligarchic one. The oligarchs sought aid from local barbarian tribes and began to wage an insurgency to get their city back. Finding itself in need of foreign aid, the popular party asked for help from the mother country, but Corcyra refused. The popular party then sought aid from Corinth, which had established Corcyra originally as its own colony and now deeply resented it for taking an independent, isolationist foreign policy—that is, for rejecting Corinth's traditional hegemony in northwestern Greece (1.25). Probably as a way to restore that hegemony, Corinth was all too happy to help the popular party in Epidamnus, but its efforts to do so alarmed the Corcyreans. With the third-largest fleet in Greece, the Corcyreans were able to defeat Corinth, which had the second-largest fleet, and Corinth's allies at the battle of Leukimme (1.26). Humiliated, the Corinthians sought revenge and began to build a bigger navy and called on all their allies for aid, with those allies forming inside the Peloponnesian League a coalition perhaps more likely to follow the lead of Corinth than of Sparta (1.27). Seeing the naval balance turn against them, the Corcyreans appealed to Athens, the largest naval power, with an offer of an alliance.

What made their appeal an offer the Athenians could not refuse? Ideally, in their view, Corcyra and Corinth might wear out each other's navies, thus leaving Athens in a stronger position relative to both (1.49). But what if Corcyra lost? In ancient Greece, naval battles did not depend so much on sinking ships as on disabling them, often by stripping their oars.[12] The victor often gained control of the defeated belligerent's ships, towed them to port, and repaired them for combat again. If Corinth defeated Corcyra, it might gain control of all or most of the latter's navy, thus tipping the naval balance against Athens, which needed control of the sea to feed itself in wartime and raise tribute within its empire. Otherwise, with an undefeated Corcyra as an ally Athens would substantially increase its naval power, but for what purpose? Containing Corinth was surely part of the story, but so too, Thucydides made clear, were Italy and Sicily, not as projects of immediate expansion but as somewhat vague yet highly passionate and deeply held aspirations to be achieved when opportunity knocked (1.33–36, 1.44). During the First Peloponnesian War, the Athenians had set up at Nisaea, Pegae, Achaea, and Naupactus bases that would have enabled them to expand toward the west. Fear of westward Athenian expansion was surely part of Corinth's hostility to Athens; denying Corinth the use of Corcyra as a base was also essential if Athens meant to compete with Corinth for influence in Italy and Sicily.

As the Corcyreans pointed out, an alliance with them would not violate the letter of the Thirty Year Peace. That treaty prohibited Athens and Sparta from poaching members of each other's alliance, but since Corcyra had been neutral and isolationist, genuinely impartial arbitration would not prove Athens had violated the treaty. So an alliance with Corcyra gave Athens the chance of gaining the fruits of a major military victory without giving the Peloponnesians a legitimate cause of war (1.35). Athenian diplomacy under Pericles thus appears to have been following a Sun Tzuian strategy to "subdue the enemy without fighting," an approach that the Eastern sage called the "acme of skill," more so even than winning "a hundred battles."[13] Although the Athenians initially rejected the offer of an alliance, in a subsequent assembly meeting they accepted a merely defensive arrangement, supplying strict rules of engagement to their commanders not to interfere in Corcyra's war with Corinth unless Corcyra itself was endangered. In theory, the defensive alliance would deter Corinth, thus giving Athens the fruits of military victory without war. This was a diplomatic gamble with high rewards but no less high risks. If Corinth was in fact deterred by the Athenian alliance with Corcyra, escalation would stop and Athens' position in western Greece would improve enormously. Athens would have taken a huge step toward revising the Thirty Year Peace without having to fight a war. Unfortunately for Athens, Corinth was not deterred and began to succeed against its former colony. Corinth began to win a naval battle at Sybota, thus drawing the Athenian navy into combat to save Corcyra's navy, in turn making possible escalation to a great-power war with Corinth's ally, Sparta (1.44–54).[14]

Still, there was no declared war yet. In part because Corinth relied on "volunteers," this conflict was still seen as a private one between Corcyra and Corinth, not between the rival alliances (1.26). Yet it would be wrong to say the Second Peloponnesian War had not yet begun. The Corinthians warned the Athenians that an alliance with Corcyra would mean war with them and eventually their allies (1.42). Thinking such war was inevitable, many Athenians thought it best for war to begin with Corcyra as an ally rather than a neutral vulnerable to Corinth (1.40–42, 1.44). True to their word, the Corinthians began to sponsor a rebellion in Athens' tribute-paying ally Potidaea. Once again, in an exercise of "plausible deniability," Corinth sent volunteers, so no one could say it was directing the affair and dragging the Peloponnesian League into a major war. Significantly, representatives from Potidaea convinced the Spartan authorities to promise to invade Attica once their rebellion began (1.58). The Spartans' promise put their credibility at stake, with huge implications for the viability of the Peloponnesian League.

From this perspective, the famous debate in Sparta that in Thucydides's narrative followed immediately on these events looks like a controversy less about whether to go to war than whether to escalate an ongoing war.[15] After all, the Spartans were planning on invading Attica even before the debate began, thus helping us understand why Thucydides believed the stated grievances in the debates were not as important as the underlying causes of the war. Corinthian representatives present egged on the Spartans, arguing that the entire balance of power, understood in social as well as geopolitical terms, was tipping against them: Spartans had to act soon, before it was too late to check the Athenians, whose diplomatic gamble all sides' leaders understood completely (1.70–71). Just in case the Spartans did not get the point, however, the Corinthians concluded their speech with a demand that Sparta "assist your allies and Potidaea, in particular, as you promised, by a speedy invasion of Attica" and "not sacrifice friends and kindred to their bitterest enemies, and drive the rest of us in despair to some other alliance" (1.71). This threat to leave the Peloponnesian League may have been hollow, but apparently the Spartans did not think they could afford to call the Corinthians' bluff, perhaps especially since the Corinthians suggested they would take other allies with them.

Ironically, the unnamed Athenian envoys whose speech followed the Corinthians' probably only fanned the flames of war in Sparta, though that was not their intent. They meant to show the power of Athens and thus to deter the Spartans; instead, their speech proved highly provocative. They declared that the Athenians were compelled by the three strongest passions in human nature (fear, honor, and interest) to acquire their empire, sustain it, and expand it. Anyone else, they claimed, would have done the same thing, for "it has always been the law that the weaker should be subject to the stronger" (1.76). If Corinth was right to argue that Athens' power was growing rapidly—through the alliance with Corcyra, for example—the envoys' defense of the Athenian empire merely proved the danger it posed to the weak, whom it would subject when opportunity was ripe. Not for the last time, the Athenians, by frank presentation of *Machtpolitik*, undermined their diplomatic objectives. Quite unintentionally, they confirmed the worst nightmares of everyone present. Because they thought it was natural and inevitable for the strong to rule the weak, the Athenians would expand until they met equal or superior strength, thus also confirming the Corinthian envoys' portrait of the Athenians as a people "who were born into the world to take no rest themselves and give none to others" (1.70). Not surprisingly, then, the majority of Spartans at the assembly voted that the "Athenians were open aggressors, and that war must be declared at once" (1.79).

Still, the Spartan king Archidamus, who was "reputed to be wise and moderate," tried to prevent further escalation, if only because the moment was not auspicious, not least from the diplomatic and legal points of view. The Athenians had concluded their speech by warning the Spartans not to break the treaty or violate their oaths but to go to arbitration first, thus suggesting the Spartans would otherwise assume responsibility for violating the peace (1.78). Archidamus did not want that responsibility without sufficient moral and legal justification, however. It might prove difficult to sustain support for the war within Sparta and among its allies, and to whatever extent he may have been pious, he might have wondered about the reaction of the gods. Indeed, Thucydides reports much later, doubts that Sparta had a just cause for the war or that it had begun in a just manner (in a surprise attack on Plataea by Thebes, a Spartan ally) had a detrimental impact on Spartan morale for much of the war. The Spartans actually believed they deserved their misfortunes, that the gods were punishing them for their injustice (1.85, 6.105, 7.18).

So Archidamus now tried to delay offensive action until the Spartans had a better pretext for war, meanwhile gathering allies among both Greeks and barbarians, raising money, and developing some form of naval power—to buy time for a long war in multiple theaters that he did not think Sparta could win with the resources and justification at hand (1.80–82). That he feared the Spartans might leave the war as a "legacy to our children" should give the lie to all claims that he at least expected to win quickly through a battle of annihilation on land (1.81). Invading Attica could aid allies like Corinth and Potidaea but was unlikely to win the war. He had to order early invasions of Attica, yet he doubted they would prove decisive. He "hoped" the Athenians would commit the blunder of fighting the invaders outside their walls (2.20), though his first speech explained that such a hope was entirely unrealistic: "Never let us be elated by the fatal hope of the war being quickly ended by a devastation of their lands" (1.81).

In light of Corinth's threat to defect from the Peloponnesian League unless Sparta took "speedy" action (1.71), however, the king's reputation for wisdom in this particular case appears to exceed his actual merits. Archidamus had a clear grasp of the likely stalemate the war would produce, Sparta's need for foreign aid (from Persia especially), and Sparta's need to acquire naval power to inspire revolts among Athenian allies so as to break the likely stalemate—all of which would take time (1.82–83). Yet it was the Spartan *ephor* (elected leader) Sthenelaidas, who comes off as an angry demagogue, who got the Corinthian message completely. It was "put up or shut up" time. The Spartans could "neither allow the further aggrandizement of Athens, nor betray our allies to ruin," because the surest way by which Athens could expand was by picking off Sparta's allies one by one (1.86).

If Athenian strategy was to destroy the Peloponnesian League, the best strategy for Sparta was to defend the league by keeping its promises to its allies, before it lost them, even if that meant going to war before Sparta was fully prepared. Such, at least, was Thucydides's view: "The growth of Athenian power could no longer be ignored" by the Spartans, because "their own confederacy became the object of its encroachments" (1.118). The problem was that Sparta's fear was not a sufficient legal or moral rationale for war, which helps to explain the fumbling and hilarious way in which the Spartans sought to make the struggle a holy war, so to speak. They demanded that the Athenians "cast out the curse" of a goddess the Athenians were said to have offended (1.126). Deftly, the Athenians under Pericles, who was implicated by ancestry in the curse and was unwilling to give up the leverage of arbitration, refused to give the Spartans a religious pretext for war and told them to cast out their own curse (1.128).

Thucydides did not say all we would like to know about the origins of the Second Peloponnesian War. In particular, he said little or nothing about the character and strength of parties in both Athens and Sparta for and against revising the Thirty Year Peace, though there is evidence they existed. The problem is that estimating their influence can be only a matter of speculation, especially in Sparta, for which written records are few.[16] Nonetheless, Thucydides succeeded in demonstrating that there was more than ample reason for Sparta to fear the growth of Athenian power enough to be willing to go to war, which was his primary purpose. Not only was Athens a de facto island, invulnerable to Spartan land power. Not only did every day of peace favor Athens, as it became stronger through wealth and tribute. Not only did each passing day give the Athenians time to build ever more ships and train crews to project their power wherever their ships could go. Not only had the Athenians announced publicly that they considered it natural and inevitable for the strong to rule the weak, with the implication that they would rule wherever they were strong. Not only had the Athenians crushed rebels, like Thasos and Samos, time and time again, thus demonstrating what would happen to the victims of their power. Not only had the Athenians used the letter of the arbitration clause in the Thirty Year Peace to undermine the spirit of the treaty and to expand to Corcyra and potentially far beyond in the west, where no one in the Peloponnesian League had ever intended they should go. They had also crossed a red line, by putting such pressure on Spartan allies, Corinth and its followers, that Sparta had to go to war to aid them or risk having fewer allies or even none at all. At that point even its marvelous hoplite army might prove vulnerable to an expanded Athenian alliance, including perhaps some of Sparta's most important traditional allies.

II

Thucydides's stress on Sparta's fear of losing allies is essential to understanding each side's war aims, the strategies each developed pursuant to them, and why it would be extraordinarily difficult for either side to make a peace it regarded as final. Sparta had both minimum and maximum goals, which correspond loosely to what Clausewitzians call "limited" and "unlimited" war objectives.[17] Sparta's immediate and minimum objective was to save its alliance by aiding its allies, who might be appeased if Sparta persuaded Athens to leave them alone and return to something like the Thirty Year Peace. This explains why lifting the siege of Potidaea and repealing the Megarian decree, which denied the Megarians the ability to trade with the Delian League, were part of the Spartan ultimatums and pretexts for war (1.139). If Athens complied, Sparta could satisfy its allies without fighting Athens. If possible, however, Sparta aimed also to "break" the power of Athens, which would require Athens to "let the Hellenes be independent" (1.118, 1.139). This final ultimatum escalated from the more moderate ones regarding Megara, Potidaea, and Aegina and from earlier religious pretexts for war. Compliance would require the Athenians to disband the Delian League, which would reverse the previous peace settlement to the status quo before the Persian Wars, when Sparta had been the clear hegemon in Greece—an ambitious objective for which Sparta and its allies clearly and simply lacked the means. As a pretext for war, demanding that Athens free the Greeks was nonetheless useful strategically for Sparta. Freeing the Greeks was most certainly as much public diplomacy, or what we today call "strategic communication," as an objective for Sparta. All Greeks, except the Athenians, could be united behind freeing other Greeks from Athens. Like the Atlantic Charter in World War II, this slogan expressed principles enormously helpful for building an extended coalition in a protracted multitheater war and bought Sparta much sympathy as the liberator of Greece throughout the Hellenic world (2.8).

At a minimum, Sparta had to stop Athens from poaching on its allies. In the best case, however, it would seek to overthrow the Athenian empire—but how? As the king of Siam says in the Broadway musical *The King and I,* that "is a puzzlement." For all the reasons explained by Archidamus previously, Sparta had no direct way of challenging Athenian power. Secure behind the walls, able to feed themselves by sea, and with a navy to ensure the allies did their bidding and paid their dues, the Athenians could wage a protracted war, even indefinitely. They could wait the Spartans out. All Sparta would be able to do would be to invade Attica, which the Athenians, since the time of Themistocles, had been willing to give up until the invader went home. As Archidamus understood, Spartan victory would depend on things and events Spartans could not control and over which they had little influence: ships and money from allies, including cities in Sicily and Italy and the Persians (who were unlikely to intervene as long as Athens was dominant at sea); rebellions within the Delian League; and above all else, Athenian mistakes, which Pericles was determined to prevent (1.82–83). All of Sparta's prospects were based on hope, though hope is not a strategy. Obliged to save their alliance, the Spartans were trapped in the most unenviable position—they would have to prosecute a war without a clear strategy for victory, pouncing when opportunity arose, which, given the slow and ponderous character of Spartans, was almost as unlikely as Athenian errors that would give the Spartans the opportunity to win (1.70, 2.65).

As for the Athenians, their immediate and minimum aims were cautious, their ultimate and maximum ones grandiose, indeed simply utopian. Their aims reflect the character of the Athenian statesman Pericles, who sought great things through calibrated measures (though the tension between his ambition and his caution has led to a great deal of confusion about his strategy, especially among those who study strategy professionally). As Platias and Koliopoulos observe, there is a difference between strategy proper, primarily dealing with military activity, which is the principal subject of Clausewitz, and grand strategy, including the usual diplomatic, economic, and intelligence activities by which states seek to achieve their objectives before, during, and after actual hostilities, a subject Sun Tzu investigated somewhat more.[18] Most accounts of Pericles as a strategist focus on his minimum objective to hold on to the Athenian empire, but offer a merely military conception of his strategy. They stress how he employed the Athenian army and navy once hostilities broke out and conclude that he meant to wage a strategy of exhaustion. From this point of view, he meant to win by not losing, holding out behind the walls of Athens, maintaining control of the sea, avoiding direct battle with Peloponnesian ground forces of equal or greater strength, keeping the Peloponnesians off balance and lifting morale at home with raids on the Peloponnesus, and avoiding new wars of conquest while still at war with Sparta and the Peloponnesian League.[19]

What is left out of this approach is the diplomacy by which especially Pericles meant not merely to preserve but also to grow the Athenian empire.[20] Without that component, accounts of Pericles's strategy are one-sided, cartoon-like caricatures of the real thing. Without attention to Pericles's prewar diplomacy, his military strategy is disconnected from his grand strategy in such a way as to obscure his ultimate objectives and how he meant to achieve them. The lesson that Pericles took from the First Peloponnesian War was, not to refrain from further expansion when circumstances permitted, but to avoid the blunders Athens had made in the first round by ensuring above all else that Athens did not get overextended. In other words, it was not policy but strategy that he meant to change.

Among other things, this change included the use of diplomacy, often seen as an alternative to war, as a continuation of war by other means. This applied especially to the requirement in the Thirty Year Peace treaty that quarrels between the Delian and Peloponnesian Leagues be settled by arbitration, with a "legalistic interpretation of the arbitration clause to disguise an Athenian bid for domination."[21] Thucydides's distinction between the stated and truest causes of the war is, among other things, an admonition to beware statesmen who, often because their motives are not publicly defensible, conceal them. Ironically, just as Sparta disguised a defensive war to preserve its alliance as an offensive war to free the Greeks, so too did Athens under Pericles disguise an offensive diplomatic initiative to expand the empire as a defensive effort to preserve the Thirty Year Peace. Academic realists have often admired Thucydides for stressing Sparta's fear of Athens' growth, but a genuine realist, paying attention to what Clausewitz called the "moral factors" (which he claimed constituted more than half of real strength), must take his hat off to Thucydides for showing how and why both sides considered it necessary at least to appear to hold the moral high ground.[22]

Precisely because Athens had not violated the letter of the Thirty Year Peace in allying with Corcyra, Pericles knew Athens was unlikely to lose in any impartial effort to settle the disputes through arbitration. Because the alliance was not compatible with the spirit of the treaty, however, it was also entirely predictable that Corinth would seek Spartan aid in response. Whether Sparta went to war or not, Athens had a good chance to break out of the containment against westward expansion established under the Thirty Year Peace. Since Pericles was no fool, he must have assumed Corinth would threaten to defect unless Sparta went to war. If Corinth left the Peloponnesian League, Athenian power relative to the Peloponnesian League (Pericles's primary adversary) would grow diplomatically, not merely through the alliance with Corcyra but also by dividing Sparta from Corinth, its chief and wealthiest ally and the only one with a significant navy, and, not least important, by reducing its access to northern Greece. If Sparta and the other Peloponnesian cities did go to war against Athens, however, but proved incapable of aiding Corinth effectively against Corcyra and Sparta so found itself compelled to make peace at some later date, Athens might still succeed at dividing the Peloponnesians. There was a good chance that not merely Corinth but also other important Spartan allies, like Thebes and Megara, would find Sparta useless for their own purposes. They might even feel betrayed by Sparta, as in fact they would immediately after the Peace of Nicias, and begin to form their own alliance, possibly including Argos, leaving Sparta so distracted by the shifting balance of power inside the Peloponnesus that it would be unable to act outside of it (5.22, 5.27).

So whether the conflict was settled through arbitration, which was preferable, or through war, which was acceptable, Athens could retain Corcyra, build a chain of bases in and outside the Crisaean Gulf to get to Corcyra, and have secure communications to and from Italy and Sicily. All Athens had to do to break up the Peloponnesian League and escape from its containment was outlast Spartan will to wage war, though it might shorten the length of time it could take Sparta to sue for peace with a judicious mix of defensive and offensive operations.

The problem is that Pericles did not explain his grand strategy publicly, though he did state publicly that that there was more to what he was doing than he was willing to say in the Athenian assembly. He had many reasons to "hope for a favorable outcome," provided Athens did not make the same mistakes as in the First

Peloponnesian War, but, he said, he would explain his reasons later in "another speech," meaning one has to look at all of his speeches to grasp the totality of his strategy. So we do not have to suspect that Pericles was keeping some cards close to his vest—he actually said so (1.144). When a statesman of his caliber deliberately informs his audience he is being discreet, one needs to treat him seriously. To grasp his strategic vision one must look as much at what he does in power as at what he says. Indeed, even Pericles's public remarks about his merely military strategy do not explain all he had in mind, perhaps because he did not wish to broadcast his intentions to enemies abroad and rivals at home on the very eve of the war. In his first speech, he still sought to win without fighting by demanding that the Peloponnesians settle through arbitration the totality of matters in dispute (1.140, 1.144). That totality (from the Athenian viewpoint, expanding via Corcyra, securing the empire against revolt at Potidaea, pressuring Megara to defect to the Delian League through economic sanctions, etc.), however, was so important that, he argued, the Athenians should accept the risk that the Peloponnesians would go to war rather than submit to their ultimatums. As a result, he stressed Athenian strengths more than weaknesses in his first speech. For all the reasons seen by Archidamus, he understood that Sparta and its allies had no direct way to overthrow Athens. The strategy of defense by land and offense by sea, which Pericles had inherited from Themistocles, meant that Athens could repel repeated invasions by land, control its allies, and launch attacks all around the Peloponnesus at targets of opportunity (1.93, 1.142).

Although these early Athenian offensive operations are often dismissed as mere raids, there has been, in the language of the *9/11 Commission Report,* a substantial failure of strategic imagination, a huge failure to "connect the dots" to construct a strategic pattern underlying these operations.[23] Consistent with Pericles's caution, if Athenian invaders got into trouble on land they could withdraw by sea, so they could always limit their losses, as Wellington did in Iberia during the Napoleonic Wars. Also, if only because they were inexperienced in operations in the Peloponnesus and hesitated to go too far inland, the Athenians were none too daring and often lost opportunities, like capturing Methone early in the war, as a result. Sooner or later, however, they might find a Spartan nerve and gain leverage for negotiations. So to understand the offensive component of Pericles's strategy of unremitting pressure on a fragile alliance, one must look at where the Athenians operated while he was still the first man in Athens and its leading strategist.

The first order of strategic business was to get Megara to flip back to the Delian League. The Athenians certainly did not fail to do so for lack of offensive spirit or action. Pericles led the largest land force in Athenian history to capture Megara in 431, the first year of the war. Sometimes Thucydides leaves out details important for understanding the strategic purpose of operations early in the war but mentions them much later. One example is that the Athenians attacked Megara twice per year, sometimes with most of their hoplite army, sometimes only with cavalry (2.31, 4.66), meaning that this was a do-or-die objective for Athens, which had only itself to blame for the long walls that enabled Megara to resist repeated assaults. In the eighth year of the war, partly with the aid of a fifth column, the Athenians took Megara's port at Nisaea and came within days, hours, or even minutes of taking the city too (4.69). Had they succeeded, they would have reversed much of the result of the First Peloponnesian War (and prevented Brasidas from leading his daring Spartan expedition to Chalcidice). Attica would have been safe from invasion, Sparta divided from Thebes, Athens enabled to expand through the Crisaean Gulf, and Corinth howling mad, perhaps even angry enough to carry out its threat to defect from the Spartan alliance.

Under Pericles the Athenians experimented, tentatively, with several other options as well. In the second year of the war Pericles led a hundred Athenian ships, fifty allied ships, four thousand hoplites, and three hundred cavalry to Epidaurus. They ravaged the territory, as usual, but also had "hopes of taking the city by assault" (2.56). This operation failed; the Epidaurians closed their gates and the Athenians left in a hurry, perhaps for fear of the arrival of Spartan ground forces. Still, the failed operation points toward a more imaginative strategy than commonly ascribed to Pericles. Once again, Thucydides does not make clear the strategic purpose of this operation when it happened. One has to connect the dots. In the thirteenth year of the war, Argos sought to capture Epidaurus for the explicit purpose of ensuring the neutrality of Corinth and giving the Athenians "shorter passage for their reinforcements" (5.55) to Argos, meaning Argos and Athens understood that Epidaurus was vital for joining their forces against Sparta and neutralizing Corinth. Had Athens taken Epidaurus, the Athenian-Argive alliance that almost defeated Sparta in 418 might well have begun in the second, not the fourteenth, year of the war, with Pericles rather than Alcibiades in command and no Nicias to obstruct going for the Spartan jugular or forcing Corinth out of the war.

As Pericles had suggested before the war, the Athenians could also fortify a base, whether at Methone (while he was still alive), at Pylos (after his death), or elsewhere in Sparta, to support a revolt of the Helots, with essential aid from the Messenian exiles at Naupactus (1.142, 2.25, 4.3–15). This would force Sparta into a two-front war, which, given its relative poverty, it could afford much less than Athens. Under Pericles, the Athenians also sought to bottle up Corinth and secure their lines of communications to Corcyra and beyond by gaining control of low-hanging fruit—islands off the coast of the Peloponnesus like Zacynthus and Cephallenia (2.7), thus adding pressure on Corinth to go its own way and leave Sparta in the lurch. Certainly to secure their rear, but perhaps also to obtain much-needed new ground forces, the Athenians under Pericles also allied with both the Macedonians and the Thracians (2.29), though they turned out to be unreliable to say the least.

It is not at all surprising that these early efforts to seize the strategic initiative were operational failures, or conversely, that the Spartans were slow to compete with the Athenians at sea, where the Athenians had the upper hand. Each side was experimenting, cautiously, with fighting in its opponent's element. The Athenians were learning on the fly how to operate in hostile Peloponnesian territory at a time when the prestige of Sparta's hoplite army was near its peak. Had some or all of these operations panned out while Pericles was still alive, however, the Spartans might well have had to negotiate peace, and the Athenians could have asked for some or all of the gains they had lost under the Thirty Year Peace—Nisaea, Pegae, Troezen, and Achaea—as Cleon would later do when the fortunes of war turned more in Athenian favor (4.21). The Second Peloponnesian War would have overturned the settlement of the first. If it had, the route to expansion in the west would have been clear. Operational failure, in other words, is no proof of a failure of strategic imagination on the part of Pericles. As is true also of the failure of the Spartans to use their fledgling navy effectively to support revolts against Athens on the island of Lesbos (3.25–35), operational failure was simply the most likely beginning in the asymmetric struggle between Athenian sea and Spartan land power, when neither side had either the confidence, the experience, or the commanders to gain decisive results.

Pericles's ultimate objectives were substantially more ambitious than most students of strategy today are wont to admit. Virtually unlimited expansion was not on the minds only of the Athenians under Pericles when they made the alliance with Corcyra, with Italy and Sicily the ultimate prize. It was emphatically part of Pericles's ambition too. This war escalates not merely militarily but also rhetorically. Pericles's first speech is cautious; his second proud, defiant, and hubristic; his last over the top in a manner that explains why his ward Alcibiades, despite his recklessness, was Pericles's natural heir, the one who best understood that Pericles along with many others had been thinking about Italy and Sicily from the beginning, just not ready to go west until he had broken up the Peloponnesian League.

In Pericles's final speech to the Athenians he put on the table some of the cards he had refused to show in his first speech. With the Athenians suffering from plague and clamoring for peace, he sought to bolster their spirits. He chose to "reveal an advantage arising from the greatness of your dominion, which I think has never suggested itself to you"—or apparently many students of this war either—"and which I never mentioned in my previous speeches." The "visible field of action" in the war had "two parts, land and sea. In the whole of one of these, you are completely supreme, not merely as far as you use it at present, but also to what further extent you may think fit: in fine, your naval resources are such that your naval vessels may go anywhere they please, without the King" of Persia "or any other nation being able to stop them" (2.62). That was how Pericles sought to prevent the Athenians from making a premature peace in a moment of weakness, by dangling the opportunity of unlimited maritime empire before them. It was because of this seemingly unlimited ability to go anywhere in the Mediterranean world by sea that the Athenians "held rule over more Hellenes than any other Hellenic state." Not merely to hold such rule but to gain more of it, and with it "the greatest name in the world," a name that would live forever, was the ultimate goal of Periclean policy and strategy (2.64).

Such a goal might seem preposterous to modern Americans, whose democratic ethos makes them uncomfortable with and suspicious of those who wear their desire for glory on their sleeves. Since the age of George Washington, Americans have preferred that their statesmen and generals cloak their ambition, however great, with humility. Worse still, Clausewitz's effort to understand war as it ought to be, as a potentially rational human endeavor, sometimes inclines strategists who have learned from him to ignore war as it often is, the product of deeply irrational forces in human nature, including the ancient desire to prove superiority to everyone else and thereby gain a kind of immortality through fame. In that way, both the modern democratic ethos and the Clausewitzian approach to politics and war can combine to blind us to the true objectives of belligerents, for any account of war in the ancient Greek world from the age of Homer to Alexander the Great that leaves out honor, fame, and glory as motives of both leaders and citizens is inconsistent with what it meant to be Greek.

In that way our ethos and our analytical tools can lead us to fail to understand the true character of the conflict, though Clausewitz himself claimed that gaining such understanding is the first, the supreme, the farthest-reaching act of judgment for any war, the one essential to understanding everything else.[24] So an idealized version of Clausewitz applied as a template to Thucydides can wind up distorting the latter's account, turning it into what we think it ought to be, not what it was in fact. The problem is not in Clausewitz but in his readers' failure to understand Thucydides on his own terms. To avoid distorting the war to suit our times and our ways of studying strategy, we have to get beyond how we today respond to the call to glory. We have to understand the deadly seriousness of Pericles in expressing, quintessentially, the ruling passion for power and glory among the Greeks.[25]

Thucydides concluded his eulogy of Pericles by stressing the "easy triumph" Pericles foresaw over the "unaided forces of the Peloponnesians," meaning that Pericles's strategy was to deal with the Peloponnesians first, others later (2.65).

His confidence was not unfounded. So long as he could prevent third-party intervention, he had grounds to think the Peloponnesian League would crumble over time. Under no circumstances did he want a war with the Peloponnesians and with other powers—like Egypt, Persia, or Sicily—at the same time, which would have been to repeat the great blunder of the First Peloponnesian War. Pericles towers above his successors not because Thucydides had unlimited regard for him or failed to recognize something deeply flawed and highly unstable in his unique blend of caution and ambition. The only statesman or general who receives anything like unlimited praise from Thucydides is Themistocles, the founder of the strategy of defense by land and offense by sea (1.138); Pericles was not in the same league. But Pericles was unlikely, had he not died in 429, to have tried to expand the empire until his strategy to break up the Peloponnesian League was fully accomplished—that is, until it would have been possible to expand in relative safety from the threat of a multifront war.

Nonetheless, Pericles's grand vision of a Mediterranean empire was utopian, for the simple reason that tiny Athens could never generate the resources required to preserve maritime hegemony in the Mediterranean Sea even if it gained it.[26] The more Athens expanded, the weaker it would become and the more vulnerable it would be to efforts by Sparta or some other power to tie it down in a multitheater war. Indeed, even the cautious side of Pericles's strategy, based on outlasting Sparta, was almost equally utopian, because the Athenians, who could neither rest nor give rest to others, were the wrong people to execute it, if any people could have. Retreating behind walls called for qualities of character inconsistent with Athenian society and culture, perhaps even with human nature itself. The Athenians, a people of seemingly limitless enterprise and energy, could not be patient. Pericles had enormous difficulty preventing them from fighting in open battle outside the city's walls, where they were almost certain to be defeated by the superior Spartans and their allies (2.21). He had even greater difficulty convincing them not to make a premature peace during the plague, which may have killed almost a third of the Athenian people. When Pericles himself died of the plague, his successors—each quarreling over different pieces of the strategy, with some, like Nicias, embracing his caution and others, like Cleon and Alcibiades, seeking to fulfill his grandiose ambition—proved incapable of putting Humpty-Dumpty back together again (2.65).

III

In light of these policies and strategies within Sparta and Athens, it was going to be very difficult to bring the Second Peloponnesian War to an end, and not for want of trying. To see why, consider three different Thucydidean accounts of war termination between Athens and the Peloponnesians in the Second

Peloponnesian War. The first attempt occurred during the plague, when Athens was down but not out; the second after Athenian victories at Pylos and Sphacteria, when Sparta in its turn was down but, again, not out. The last occurred after the Spartan victories in Chalcidice, at Amphipolis especially, and Athenian defeat on land in Boeotia at the battle of Delium. In the last instance both sides were down, but each had some leverage over the other and so could bargain and negotiate.

In contrast to his ample detail about the symptoms of the plague in Athens, Thucydides is surprisingly reticent about the peace talks for which the plague was the major contributing cause. Thucydides introduces his account of the plague immediately after Pericles's Funeral Oration, itself noteworthy for present purposes for its discussion of the accomplishments and ambitions of different Athenian generations and for its demands on Athenian women, mothers especially. Pericles called attention to the grandparents in his audience, the ones who had fought at Marathon and Salamis, thus saving Greece—perhaps all of Europe—from Persian rule. He also called attention to the parents in his audience, the ones who had established the Athenian empire throughout the Aegean (2.36).

His central theme, however, was the current generation of Athenians and the beauty, nobility, power, and greatness of their city, including (but by no means limited to) their free way of life. What could the younger generation do to equal or surpass its ancestors? Since the subject of the Funeral Oration was not democracy as such but the fame of being an Athenian, and thus the immortality of name that might compensate for mortality in combat, that question needed to be addressed. Great things do not come from puny efforts. As Pericles had said earlier (1.143), the Athenians could not pine over the loss of their homes and farms and ancestral gods as the Spartans ravaged Attica. Merely to equal the heroes of Salamis they would have to be willing to abandon all these things, as Themistocles had advised them to do when he developed the strategy of the long walls (1.93). They would have to understand that when Athenians died in battle they gained immortality. Hence, the few (so far) who had fallen in combat "received the renown which never grows old, and for a tomb, not so much that in which their bodies have been deposited, but that noblest of shrines wherein their glory is laid up to be eternally remembered upon every occasion on which deed or story shall be commemorated" (2.43). Since they had purchased immortality with their lives, their sacrifices were not losses at all but gains for themselves as individuals and for Athenians collectively.

Significantly, if any Athenian desired glory beyond that of his grandparents and his parents, it would not be enough to preserve what had already been acquired. As Abraham Lincoln explained at the Springfield Young Men's Lyceum in 1838, the young may earn respect but not glory by perpetuating the accomplishments of their forebears. The most ambitious, the ones who belong to "the family of the lion" and "the tribe of the eagle"—like Alexander, Caesar, Napoleon, and, one must add, Alcibiades—aspire to much more than perpetuating other people's glory. "Towering genius disdains a beaten path. It seeks regions hitherto unexplored. It sees *no distinction* in adding story to story, upon the monuments of fame, erected in the memory of others. . . . It *scorns* to tread in the footsteps of *any* predecessor, however illustrious. It thirsts and burns for distinction; and if possible, it will have it, whether at the expense of emancipating slaves [Lincoln's eventual role] or enslaving freemen [the role the Athenians chose]."[27] Greeks were agonistic (that is, competitive), especially with each other, and especially for that highest term of praise in Homer, "godlike." If the members of the current generation were to engage in a competition with each other, and with their ancestors, to be like the gods, they would have to go and do something significant where no Athenian had gone or done anything remarkable before, which would not be easy. Pericles boasted that they had already "forced every sea and land to be the highway of our daring, and everywhere, whether for good [to friends] or evil [to enemies], have left imperishable monuments behind us" (2.41).

Their parents had already built the empire in the east. So the best chance of earning immortal fame for the current generation was in gaining an empire in the west—that is, in revising the Thirty Year Peace on terms that in time might more than double the size of the Athenian empire. Such an accomplishment would more than compensate for the casualties; indeed, even if Athens failed, it might earn glory merely for having braved so much. "Comfort, therefore, not condolence," is what Pericles had to offer the parents of the dead, for "fortunate indeed are they who draw for their lot a death so glorious as that which caused [their parents'] mourning" (2.44). In light of that good fortune, the best that could be done, by those capable of it, for the dead, for themselves, and for Athens, whose interests were presumably all in harmony, was to have more children, who could grow up to fight for Athens and continue the cycle of aspiring for glory, to be like the gods, by risking all in combat—that is, through endless war (2.44). Perhaps unintentionally, and quite tragically, Pericles, whose strategy depended on calibrated steps toward a larger goal, in the Funeral Oration found it necessary to boost morale by getting the Athenians drunk on ambition. The elder statesman could hold his liquor, but not his younger successors.

The plague did not show up in Athens an hour, a day, or a week after Pericles gave this challenge to Athenians to gain immortal fame in endless competition; it came half a year later. But Thucydides deliberately inserted his account of the plague immediately after the speech. Perhaps the main reason Thucydides's account of the plague occurs where it does in his narrative is to remind us that there is a limit to our ability to be heroes and sacrifice for a presumably common good.

As Clausewitz observed, the sacrifices demanded in time of war can pass the culminating point of social tolerance. One reason wars never or rarely become absolutely "total" is that "in most cases a policy of maximum exertion would fail because of the domestic problems it would cause."[28] The contrast between what Pericles asked of Athenians when facing death and what they actually did when they all thought they had been sentenced to an agonizing death by disease is striking, and intentional. Among other things, Athenians ceased to care about funeral rites, sometimes having "recourse to the most shameless modes of burial," such as throwing bodies on top of funeral pyres meant for others and then running away. Perseverance "in what men call honor was popular with none, it was so uncertain they would be spared to obtain the object." The Athenians lost all "fear of gods or law of man. . . . As for the first, they judged it to be just the same whether they worshipped them or not, as they saw all alike perishing; and for the last, no one expected to live to be brought to trial for his offenses[,] . . . and before they fell it was only reasonable to enjoy life a little" (2.52–53). In times like those—apparently the "end days," as fundamentalists might say today—it was only natural for the people to swing to extremes, from irreligion and hedonism to superstition. So some consulted oracles and blamed the plague on the war and on those, like Pericles, who had convinced them, walled and crammed inside the city with little shelter (like refugees from Hurricane Katrina in the New Orleans Superdome in 2005), to accept the war rather than submit to Sparta's ultimatums.

Hawks like Pericles became increasingly unpopular as a result, but amazingly, after losing as many citizens to the plague as they were likely to have lost in a protracted war, the Athenians kept up the fight, trying to take Epidaurus, attacking Troezen, Halieis, and Hermione, and reinforcing the besiegers at Potidaea (who had also caught the plague) (2.56–57). At the same time, however, having endured perhaps more than human nature can bear, they "became eager to come to terms with Sparta, and actually sent ambassadors thither who however did not succeed in their mission" (2.59).

Thucydides does not explain the failure of this peace mission. We can make only intelligent inferences. The plague had put the Athenians in a world of pain, and the Spartans knew it. If all the Spartans had asked for was a return to the status quo ante, the fighting might have stopped, but the war would not have ended. The result would not have been final, because once the pressure of the annual invasions of Attica was off, the Athenians would have returned to their homes in the suburbs, escaped the crowding of the city, recovered their health, and (following Pericles's advice) had more children—that is, baby soldiers and sailors for the next round. Also, Sparta could not act as a free agent. Having escalated the conflict at the behest of its allies, it could not make a separate peace without risking their loss.

In any case, if the result was to be final, the Spartans had to keep the pressure on, but the nature of their maximal political demand—that Athens liberate the Hellenes by dissolving its empire—was such that the Athenians could not accept it without committing strategic suicide. As Pericles said in his third speech, when he tried to dissuade Athenians from making a premature peace, the empire might have been unjust to acquire but was imprudent to let go. "For what you hold is, to speak somewhat plainly, a tyranny; to take it perhaps was wrong; but to let it go is unsafe" (2.63). The Persians might make a comeback. Athenian allies (subjects) might seek revenge. Without allies, Athens would have had no tribute to fund its navy and no trade to feed itself if the Peloponnesians renewed the war, with bitter Corinth egging on the Spartans to seek a "final solution," such as killing all the men in Athens and selling the women and children into slavery, as indeed Corinth would propose at the very end of the war.[29] With their backs against the wall, literally on what Sun Tzu called "death ground," with no choice but to keep fighting or die, the Athenians had good reason to refuse Sparta's maximal terms.[30] Conversely, the Spartans, presumably thinking Athens was down for the count, would have had good reason to refuse possible concessions from Athens, like lifting the embargo against Megara. So long as the maximal objectives of one side were incompatible with the minimal objectives of the other, a negotiated peace was impossible. So the war went on and on and on.

Almost the inverse occurred after the great Athenian victory at Pylos. After years of trying, the Athenians struck not one but two vital nerves among the Spartans. At Pylos the Athenians had established a fortified base to support a rebellion of the Helots, thus forcing Sparta into a two-front war, with the insurgency at home inclining the Spartans to shut down the other front in Attica. At Sphacteria, an island off the coast of Pylos, the Athenians had also managed to cut off 420 Spartan hoplites, who could be supplied only by Helots swimming from the shore to the island. With these forces in danger, the Spartans made an armistice and sent an embassy to Athens offering not merely peace but an alliance (4.16–21).

Certainly, the Athenians could have had peace at this time, and a far better one than the status quo ante, but there were two fundamental obstacles. First, Cleon, the "most violent man" in Athens (3.36), did his best to sabotage the negotiations, and second, the Athenians, under the influence of Cleon, kept demanding more than Sparta could accept. The Athenians were determined to reverse the Thirty Year Peace treaty. They wanted back all that they had lost at the end of the First Peloponnesian War: Nisaea and Pegae, after the recovery of which it would probably have been only a matter of time before Megara fell and returned to the Athenian empire; Troezen, giving them a foothold on the eastern Peloponnesus near Argos, if they chose to ally with that Spartan rival in the future; and Achaea, at the western end of the Gulf of Corinth, a foothold that (along with Naupactus) would have enabled them to control all communications, military and commercial, to and from Corcyra, Italy, Sicily, and the Crisaean Gulf (4.21). Had the Spartans accepted these demands Cleon would have earned his share of immortal fame as the greatest Athenian statesman since Themistocles, even greater than Pericles, so he had important personal motives (of the sort encouraged, ironically, by Pericles in the Funeral Oration) to make such demands and continue the war until they were accepted.

Cleon's objectives were consistent with the most ambitious goals of Pericles, though he was not as cautious or nearly as diplomatic. By refusing to negotiate with the Spartans in secret, demanding rather that negotiations be conducted before the Athenian assembly, Cleon was using a Wilsonian approach, based on "open covenants openly arrived at," for anything but Wilsonian ends. Cleon put the ambassadors in an impossible situation, which may well have been his object. A public discussion of the terms meant that the Spartans, whose envoys were willing to betray their allies by an alliance with Athens, would lose face with those allies and perhaps their leadership of the Peloponnesian League. If breaking up the Peloponnesian League was still the primary Athenian objective, however, Cleon ought to have accepted the Spartan offer of an alliance, which would have pushed Corinth and its coalition inside the Peloponnesian League away from Sparta. Since a Spartan king had been suspected of taking bribes from the Athenians at the end of the First Peloponnesian War and had been exiled temporarily as a result, the Spartan negotiators knew that accepting humiliating terms from the Athenians might risk exile for themselves, or worse, when they returned home.

More lenient terms from Athens might have made a difference. Perhaps the Athenians might have negotiated for something more than just an alliance (which was unlikely to last anyway). So perhaps they needed to ask for not much more than the Spartan envoys had already offered. Had the Athenians limited their demands to Nisaea and Pegae, for example, and done this in private, perhaps the Spartan negotiators would have taken the risk of political embarrassment at home for the sake of rescuing the garrison on Sphacteria, securing the return of Pylos, and preventing future aid from Athens to rebels among the Helots. With such a concession it was highly probable that Megara would have been compelled to return to the Delian League, thus walling off all of Attica from the Peloponnesians while opening access for Athenian expansion through the Crisaean Gulf. The envoys' position had been made impossible by the nature and form of the Athenian demands, however, and they returned to Sparta. So the negotiations failed, and the war went on and on and on.

No one can know for sure whether different terms and a different way of offering them might have resulted in a treaty ending the hostilities, at least temporarily. Shortly after the botched negotiations, however, the Athenian general Demosthenes and, surprisingly, Cleon managed to defeat and capture the Spartan garrison at Sphacteria, including 120 full Spartiates, sons of the leading men in Sparta. The surrender was a severe blow to Spartan prestige. Because of the famous refusal of the three hundred Spartans to surrender to the Persians at Thermopylae, nothing in the war shocked the Greeks more than the surrender of the garrison at Sphacteria (4.38–40). The Greeks discovered that Spartans were mortal too. Moreover, the Spartans began to doubt themselves. Fearful that Helot incursions from the sanctuary at Pylos would lead to revolution at home, they ceased offensive operations outside the Peloponnesus and sent more envoys to Athens. Yet the Athenians "kept grasping for more" than the envoys could negotiate and dismissed one embassy after another (4.42). Meanwhile, the Athenians, holding hostage the prisoners taken from Sphacteria, believed they could attack almost anywhere (Corinth, the Peloponnesian coast, Anactorium, Cythera, Megara, or elsewhere) with impunity, for if they had a setback, they believed, they could always negotiate at that time from a position of strength (4.41–55).

When the tides of war shifted once again in Sparta's favor, however, the Athenians came to regret demanding more than Sparta could accept (5.14). This confirms that genuine peace, like war, must involve at least two sides. Not only must the defeated party renounce efforts to revise the terms in the future, but also the victor must refrain from demanding terms that can only make the defeated party desire to renew or escalate the conflict when opportunity permits. The victor needs to avoid reinforcing the defeated belligerent's will to resist; the defeated belligerent needs to calculate whether it can live with the victor's terms in the long run or must accept those terms only so long as they are absolutely necessary to serve some larger end.[31]

Of course, the most famous effort to terminate the war is the Peace of Nicias, appropriately named in Athens after Nicias, the Athenian statesman and general who most wanted peace, one who shared Pericles's caution but lacked his ambition for Mediterranean hegemony. He too sought personal fame, that of a peacemaker, at a time when the Athenians were willing to give peace a chance. His opportunity came from a startling upset victory by the Spartans. Leading a ragtag force of elite Spartan soldiers and Helots who had been promised freedom for their service, Brasidas, the most daring and innovative Spartan general of the war, managed to make his way from the Peloponnesus through barbarian-controlled Thessaly and Macedonia to Chalcidice, where Athens had many important tribute-paying allies, silver mines, and lumber yards to supply wood for ships. A "good speaker for a Spartan," Brasidas, somewhat like T. E. Lawrence of Arabia among the Arabs within the Ottoman Empire in the First World War, managed to convince Athenian allies that Sparta actually meant to liberate them from the Athenian empire. By promising lenient terms to those who joined Sparta against Athens, he convinced several cities to rebel, the most important being Amphipolis, a colony founded by Athens and a nerve center for the Athenians, who were in need of supplies and a secure sea line of communications to the Hellespont (4.81, 4.84, 4.106). Perhaps most important, Amphipolis was a symbol of effective resistance to the Athenian empire, which both Pericles and Cleon had called a tyranny (2.63, 3.37). So long as Amphipolis and other cities in Chalcidice remained independent, they would give hope to others that resistance to Athenian tyranny was not impossible. In other words, the independence of these cities meant a risk that the Athenian empire would fall apart.

Having set this sword of Damocles hanging over the heads of the Athenians, the Spartans opened negotiations with them and achieved a one-year armistice (4.117). However, Brasidas—the glory of liberating these cities having perhaps gone to his head—disregarded and disobeyed orders not to prosecute further hostilities (4.135), putting his operations increasingly in conflict with the Spartans' current political objective of a negotiated peace. So it was probably a stroke of good fortune for Sparta's peace party that he, the best Spartan general of the war, and Cleon, the most bloodthirsty Athenian general (who, Thucydides said, needed the war to continue to distract attention from his crimes and slanders against his political opponents in Athens), were both killed in combat at Amphipolis (5.10). The most prominent proponents of the war on both sides were dead, thus enabling a change of leadership and a change of political objectives, at least temporarily, with both Athens and Sparta willing to settle for minimum objectives (5.16).

Both sides had powerful but unequal motives to end hostilities. The Athenians needed Amphipolis back to stem the tide of revolt among their allies, and, having suffered a punishing defeat at Delium, especially, they had lost the confidence that had once led them to take the offensive almost everywhere. The Spartans had come to understand that their original strategy of devastating Athenian territory and supporting allies in a multitheater war could neither bait the Athenians to fight them outside the walls of Athens nor overthrow the maritime empire that enabled Athens to continue the fight. The surrender of the soldiers at Sphacteria was a disaster "hitherto unknown" in Sparta; Spartan lands were being plundered from Pylos and Cythera; and the Helots were deserting their farms for the insurgents, whose attacks tied down much of the Spartan army. Sparta feared that free Helots from outside Sparta would join forces with those inside. Perhaps most importantly, Sparta's treaty with Argos, another treaty with an expiration date, was about to end, meaning it might soon have to fight Athens, Argos, the Helots, and any others who might wish to join the fray, all at the same time (5.14).

With new leaders in Sparta and Athens, a compromise was possible. In Athens, Nicias, who counted himself lucky to be successful so far, wished "while still happy and honored, . . . to secure his good fortune, to obtain a present release from trouble for himself and his countrymen," and to earn his own immortality. He meant to "hand down to posterity a name as an ever successful statesman" who had made a lasting peace, arguably an accomplishment greater than that of Pericles. Since he had been successful so far, and war is an affair of chances, the best way for him to win the ancient Greek equivalent of the Nobel Peace Prize was to make the peace that bears his famous name (5.15–16). For his part, the Spartan king Pleistonax, who had been accused of accepting bribes to end the First Peloponnesian War, saw an opportunity to redeem his reputation from this and other scandalous accusations. Thinking that "in peace no disaster would occur" for which he was likely to be held responsible "and that when Sparta recovered her men there would be nothing for his enemies [in Sparta] to seize upon," he too was willing to lend his name to ending active hostilities (5.17). To strengthen his negotiating position, he openly made plans not merely to invade and ravage but also to occupy Attica and garrison fortifications within it, meaning the Athenians would not be able to return to their homes and farms if he carried out his plan. So conditions were ripe to make a trade.

Under the treaty, the Athenians would get Amphipolis and other Chalcidean cities back as tribute-paying allies, provided the Athenians did not molest the citizens of those cities and allowed them to be independent. (It was unclear how Sparta could give back to Athens cities liberated by Brasidas if they objected, as they certainly would, knowing the ruthless treatment that defeated rebels, like Mytilene and Scione, usually received from Athens [3.50, 5.17–18, 5.32].) In return, the Athenians were supposed to surrender cities and places captured during the war, including Pylos, and to release any Spartan prisoners they held. Like most other treaties in Thucydides's narrative, this one came with an expiration date. It was supposed to last for fifty years, thus suggesting the irony that in Thucydides's account the further away the expiraton date of peace treaties, the less likely the peace is to endure. To ensure fidelity to the terms, each side was to swear an oath to the gods, who presumably punished oath breakers. Here is another irony of Thucydides's chronicle—it consists of the moral, intellectual, religious, and legal somersaults that would-be and actual belligerents were willing to perform to convince themselves and others that they had not violated a treaty or other convention, that the gods were not against them but actually on their side.

In other words, they were extraordinarily skillful at finding pretexts to violate their treaties, so the oaths were next to meaningless as guarantees of the peace.[32]

If Pericles's primary objective at the start of the war was to break up the Peloponnesian League, then Athens clearly won the Peace of Nicias. Sparta's principal allies—the Boeotians, the Corinthians, the Megarians, and the Eleans—refused to go along with the treaty (5.17 and 5.21), partly because it allowed Sparta and Athens to revise its terms without consulting them. These allies began to make separate arrangements with each other, thus giving Athens a god-sent diplomatic opportunity to isolate Sparta in the Peloponnesus. Rightly, however, Thucydides calls the Peace of Nicias a "treacherous armistice," not a peace (5.26). Sparta simply could not deliver on its promised terms, which were unenforceable. The Amphipolitans refused to return to the Delian League, and nothing Sparta could say would make them do so. Indeed, Sparta's own general Clearidas, seeing the treaty as an act of treachery against those whom Sparta had promised freedom, refused even to try to turn the liberated cities back to Athens (5.21). Sparta, its traditional allies having repudiated the treaty, was obliged, for fear of war with Argos, to seek a new alliance in Athens. The erstwhile enemies duly formed a fifty-year alliance pledging to wage war and make peace together and committing Athens to help Sparta put down Helot rebellions if they occurred. After signing the alliance, the Athenians gave Sparta its prisoners back, though they held on to Pylos just in case they needed it as security for the hoped-for return of Amphipolis (5.23–24).

IV

Although many in Greece believed the conflict was over, Thucydides, in retrospect, demurs. The full-scale war that followed six years later was not a separate war but a continuation of the Second Peloponnesian War, which had been a continuation of the First Peloponnesian War. In the six years of the Peace of Nicias, byzantine diplomacy carried on the unending war by other means. The (nominally) fifty-year treaty and alliance could not "be rationally considered a state of peace, as neither party either gave or got back all that they had agreed" (5.26). Added to this, numerous violations of its terms occurred, most notably the battle of Mantinea, the largest land battle of the war, pitting Athens and Argos, Athens' new ally, against Sparta. Perhaps if the Athenians had supported their new ally more effectively and instigated a Helot revolt at the same time, this could have been a decisive victory on land for the Athenians. As it was, because the Athenians were half-hearted, some wanting to finish off Sparta and others wanting to save the so-called peace, the Spartans were able to defeat the coalition and restore much of their own martial prestige (5.75). All the protection Athens now had from its enemies to the north in Boeotia was an armistice renewable every ten days (5.26).

Most importantly, the treaty did not resolve the original cause of the war—the fears in Sparta and among its allies of the growth of Athenian power. The Athenians needed a break, but they had not ceased to be ambitious to expand. If anything, the war had only fortified this hunger, a dream deferred so long that delay could no longer be tolerated. The series of treacherous diplomatic realignments during the period of official peace was as confusing as the "Who's on first?" logic of Abbott and Costello, but Sparta's original allies eventually got over Sparta's original betrayal. Fear of Athens drove them back into alliance with Sparta. The war had settled nothing, and every day without active hostilities meant that Athens was growing stronger, filling its treasury with tribute, building more ships, and training new crews for the next round—in Sicily.

The Athenians had coveted Sicily since before the Second Peloponnesian War and (contrary to Pericles's advice to avoid overextending themselves) had visited several times, even while the war back home was hot, to "test the possibility of bringing Sicily into subjection" (3.86, 3.115, 4.2, 4.24–25, 5.4). The Athenians had even fined one of the naval commanders on these missions and banished two others for allegedly taking bribes

> to depart when they might have subdued Sicily. So thoroughly had their present prosperity [after victory at Pylos] persuaded the Athenians that nothing could withstand them, and that they could achieve what was possible and impracticable alike, with means ample or inadequate it mattered not. The reason for this was their general extraordinary success, which made them confuse their strength with their hopes. (4.65)

For Thucydides, neither Pericles nor his successors, save Nicias, ever intended to renounce or even compromise their objective of establishing for Athens the greatest name, based on the greatest rule over the Greeks, an objective that pushed them toward dominating the larger Mediterranean world, and ultimately to Sicily. That ill-fated adventure did not arise from a change of policy but from a change of strategy, based on both worst-case assessments (of what might happen if Sicily united under Syracuse and aided the Peloponnesians) and best-case assessments (of Athenian prospects of success in a faraway theater on an island larger than Attica itself, with cities whose total population was larger than that of Athens) (6.1, 6.6–8). Each of these assessments was preposterous: first, Syracuse was no threat to Athens until the Athenians went to Sicily and stirred up the hornet's nest; second, the Sicilian city of Egesta, which wanted their aid against its perennial enemy Selinus, had deceived the Athenians into thinking it would pay for the expedition (6.46).

These are classic examples of how to manipulate allies or enemies into doing one's bidding, based on appealing to their worst fears and fondest hopes, though here the Athenians deceived themselves at least as much as they were deceived by others. Athenians believed that even if they failed in Sicily (in spite of the enormous power of the force they sent) Athens would suffer no harm, because of the disarray in the Peloponnesus and the so-called peace treaty with Sparta and its allies (6.24). In this they were at least partly right. It was unlikely Athens could have held whatever it conquered in Sicily, especially if Carthage intervened, but the expedition need not have led to disaster. That was the result of judgments of the ground commanders, Nicias especially, and their dysfunctional relations with the people of Athens (7.42, 7.48). Among other things, Nicias's procrastination in Sicily gave the Spartans opportunity to catch the Athenians in the grand-strategic trap they had always dreamed of—a protracted, multitheater war, with fronts both in Attica (where this time the Spartans fortified Deceleia and cut off the Athenians from their farms and mines) and in Sicily. The effort drained the Athenian treasury and compelled Athens to demand higher tribute from its allies, which encouraged those allies to rebel as soon as they got the chance (7.28). All this and more was handed the Spartans when the Athenians lost the best of their army and navy at Syracuse, thus removing much of Persia's reluctance to intervene. It was anything but inevitable that Athens would lose the war even at this late date, but it now simply could not afford to lose a decisive battle at sea and desperately needed peace to reconstitute for another round.

It is tempting to see Athens' comeuppance, not merely in Sicily but also in the war itself, as a form of divine punishment; however, Thucydides, who barely hides his skepticism about the Greek gods, gives us no reason to reach such a conclusion. Thucydides's world is ruled not by the gods or by karma; instead, it is conditioned by a natural economy of power and violence that endures today. *Hubris* and *nemesis,* whatever their religious connotations, are natural phenomena for Thucydides; they are seen time and again not only in this war but in war in general.[33] Had Athens not self-destructed in Sicily, it would have done so eventually somewhere else—in Italy or Carthage, for example—because it was drunk on the passion for power and glory. That passion, requiring continual expansion, was inculcated but not invented by Pericles in the Funeral Oration, and it found its most virulent expression in Alcibiades's speech before the Sicilian expedition (6.16–18, 6.24).[34] True, Athens did sober up in the immediate aftermath of disaster in Sicily (8.1), but again, the Athenians were born to take no rest nor to give any to others.

Although Thucydides lived through the end of the war, he did not finish his account of it. Perhaps he died, perhaps something else took priority, but other sources confirm Thucydides's characterization of the Athenians as a people incapable of making a durable peace because they could not be sated with power. After surprising comeback victories in the last years of the war, at Arginusae especially, the Athenians, thinking they were rising again, refused Spartan offers of peace on the basis of the status quo, an offer they would have accepted gladly immediately after the failed Sicilian expedition. During the fierce and confused battle at Arginusae, perhaps the largest naval battle of the war, many Athenians fell into the sea, leaving their commanders torn between saving them and pursuing the retreating Peloponnesian fleet; in the event they left ships behind to rescue the survivors, but a storm made that impossible. When the commanders returned to Athens, the Athenians did not congratulate them on their victory or take a deep breath because of the chance of peace it offered. Instead, they put on trial all eight for failing to save the drowning sailors. All were convicted, six were executed, and two fled before they were killed by the very people whose empire they had saved. Not long thereafter Athens lost its fleet, control of the sea, and ultimately the war, along with its democratic regime, at Aegospotami, through the tactical incompetence of a commander who allowed his fleet to be surprised on the beach. Surely one reason for that was that the Athenians themselves had killed or driven into exile their best admirals. If they had made peace after Arginusae, they would not have lost the war, at least not for good.[35] Yet war, says Thucydides in his account of the revolution in Corcyra, is a "rough master" (3.82). It produces what we today call PTSD, post–traumatic stress disorder, which distorts, even deranges, judgment, not merely among soldiers and sailors but among the people too. However rational the Athenians under Pericles may have appeared at the beginning of the war, they were irrational, if not truly mad, at the end—they could not make peace. Tragically, Thucydides's account from the plague to the Sicilian expedition and beyond to the revolution in Athens shows the gradual breakdown of strategic rationality in the world's most famous democracy.

For Thucydides, expansionist powers who refuse to make peace (when necessity demands and opportunity allows) create and perpetuate the sort of fear seen in Sparta and its allies, a fear that leads others to check them, if necessary, by overthrowing their regimes and establishing something fundamentally less threatening. Sparta did that to Athens after its surrender, and the grand alliance of the United States, Great Britain, and the Soviet Union of World War II did it to the Axis powers. At no place in Thucydides's account was Athens ever a sated power, but it ought to have been one, a lesson that perhaps no Greek city, least of all Athens, could ever learn. This suggests that preventing great-power war in our own time will depend on the willingness of former belligerents—like China, the United States, and their respective allies, for example—to accept the results of their previous conflicts in Korea (where there is still only an armistice) and over islands, including Taiwan, off the coast of China as final enough not to need revising by violent means.[36] They need to act like sated powers—what Athens should have been in this conflict, not what it was. Preventing great-power war in the twenty-first century will therefore depend at least as much on self-restraint as on deterrence. That is a lesson that great powers especially often fail to take away from Thucydides's "possession for all time"—his account not merely of the origins and conduct of the heartbreaking war between the Peloponnesians and the Athenians but also of their tragic failure to make a genuine peace while there was time, opportunity, and overwhelmingly good reason to do so.

NOTES

The author would like to thank Ian, Alex, and Lisa Walling; his Naval War College colleagues in Newport and Monterey; and the Gentrain Society of Monterey Peninsula College, for their criticism and support for this article.

1. Epigraphs from, respectively, Carl von Clausewitz, *On War*, ed. and trans. Michael Howard and Peter Paret (Princeton, N.J.: Princeton Univ. Press, 1984), p. 80; and Sun Tzu, *The Art of War*, trans. Samuel B. Griffith (Oxford, U.K.: Oxford Univ. Press, 1963), p. 73.

2. Unless otherwise indicated, all citations from Thucydides are from *The Landmark Thucydides: A Comprehensive Guide to the Peloponnesian War*, ed. Robert B. Strassler, trans. Richard Crawley, rev. ed. (New York: Free Press, 2006), and are given by book and paragraph—for example, 5.26 means Book V, paragraph 26.

3. Clausewitz, *On War*, p. 80.

4. That Athens was a sated power is one of Donald Kagan's major theses in *The Outbreak of the Peloponnesian War* (Ithaca, N.Y.: Cornell Univ. Press, 1969), esp. pp. 190–92, 345–47. Though many disagree with Kagan's thesis, designed to show the war was not inevitable, all must salute his remarkable accomplishment, a new critical, and deeply revisionist, four-volume history of the Peloponnesian War that took perhaps almost as long to complete as it took Thucydides to write his own uncompleted book, and without the advantage of many of Thucydides's immediate sources. Moreover, Kagan's project needs to be seen in light of the First World War and the Cold War, especially. Thinking a war is inevitable not only risks becoming a self-fulfilling prophecy but might tempt belligerents into preventive war, as some say was the case for Germany in August 1914, with the near suicide of European civilization and collapse of four great empires (those of Germany, Austria, Russia, and the Ottomans) as the consequence. In the age of massive nuclear arsenals, "inevitablist" thinking and preventive-war mind-sets of the sort made famous in the 1964 film *Dr. Strangelove* could only have made an already bad situation much, much worse. Statesmen needed to find a place for freedom of action whereby strategy could spell the difference between catastrophe and the survival of all that makes human life worth living. So Kagan's staunch defense of the possibility of statesmanship and strategy to prevent escalation to great-power war deserves enormous respect. That does not mean he was correct about Athens being a sated power, however. For other critiques of Kagan's claim, see Athanasios G. Platias and Konstantinos Koliopoulos, *Thucydides on Strategy: Grand Strategies in the Peloponnesian War and Their Relevance Today* (New York: Columbia Univ. Press, 2010), pp. 32–34; Lawrence A. Tritle, *A New History of the Peloponnesian War* (Chichester, U.K.: Wiley-Blackwell, 2010), pp. 35–39; and, with some ambivalence, Victor Davis Hanson, *A War like No Other: How the Athenians and the Spartans Fought the Peloponnesian War* (New York: Random House, 2005), pp. 12–14.

5. That is, rooted in the view of the German historian Hans Delbrueck (1848–1929), who distinguished between wars to annihilate enemy forces in decisive battles leading directly to a peace settlement and wars of attrition in

which an exhausted opponent, often fearing revolution or third-party intervention, makes peace because it believes itself unable to continue the struggle at an acceptable cost or level of risk. See, for example, Platias and Koliopoulos, *Thucydides on Strategy,* pp. 35–80.

6. In this case, the Loeb translation of this famous passage seems more useful than Richard Crawley's in the Strassler edition. Crawley and most others translate the Greek adjective Thucydides used to describe the cause of the war as "real," but it is the superlative of the Greek word *aletheia* and means "truest." What was said and done immediately before the war, especially regarding matters of law and justice, was not irrelevant to its origins—it served as a catalyst, or Aristotelian "efficient" cause. But great wars do not occur over small stakes. More fundamental and important was Sparta's fear of the growth of Athens, which put Spartan security, prestige, interests, and traditional hegemony in Greece all at risk. Significantly, Thucydides did not say the war between Athens and Sparta was "inevitable" (as Crawley and many others translate this passage), though he came close. Instead, as the Loeb translation reveals, he said the growth of Athenian power and the fear it produced in Sparta "forced," or compelled, Sparta to go to war.

The operative Greek word is *ananke,* necessity. As Clausewitz reveals, war arises from a clash of policies. The war was not inevitable if Athens renounced an expansionist foreign policy or if Sparta was willing to accept the rise of Athens rather than oppose it. But if Athens insisted on expansion and Sparta on containing it, it was only a matter of time before one or both of them gave up on its truce; see Thucydides, *History of the Peloponnesian War,* Books I and II, Loeb Classics, trans. Charles Forster Smith (Cambridge, Mass.: Harvard Univ. Press, 1991), p. 43, and Simon Hornblower, *A Commentary on Thucydides* (Oxford, U.K.: Clarendon, 1991), vol. 1 (Books I–III), pp. 64–66. For the tip of an enormous iceberg regarding the origins of the war, see also Kagan, *Outbreak of the Peloponnesian War;* Platias and Koliopoulos, *Thucydides on Strategy;* George Cawkwell, *Thucydides and the Peloponnesian War* (New York: Routledge, 1997); Robert W. Connor,

Thucydides (Princeton, N.J.: Princeton Univ. Press, 1984); Tritle, *New History of the Peloponnesian War;* and Hanson, *War like No Other.* Especially useful not merely for understanding the origins of the war but as a summary of the vast literature on Thucydides is Perez Zagorin's *Thucydides: An Introduction for the Common Reader* (Princeton, N.J.: Princeton Univ. Press, 2005).

7. Sun Tzu, *Art of War,* p. 77.

8. Scholars are uncertain of the date of the Thasian rebellion, as well as of the dates of the earthquake and Messenian rebellion in Sparta that in Thucydides's account follow on the revolt in Thasos. See Strassler, ed., *Landmark Thucydides,* p. 55.

9. Herodotus, *The Landmark Herodotus: The Histories,* ed. Robert B. Strassler, trans. Andrea L. Purvis (New York: Pantheon, 2007), 1.87.

10. See Strassler, ed., *Landmark Thucydides,* editor's note at 1.40.

11. Thucydides, *The Peloponnesian War: The Complete Hobbes Translation,* ed. David Grene, trans. Thomas Hobbes (Chicago: Chicago Univ. Press, 1989); Thomas Hobbes, *The Leviathan,* ed. C. B. McPherson (London: Penguin Books, 1968), chap. 13, pp. 183–88.

12. It is easy to imaginswe from the image on the cover of this issue the damage that might be done to a trireme's oars and oarsmen by an adversary (its own oars momentarily "shipped," drawn into the hull as far as possible) passing close aboard and driving through the three banks.

13. Sun Tzu, *Art of War,* p. 77.

14. Following Plutarch (*Pericles,* 29.3), Donald Kagan suggests that the clash of the Athenian and Corinthian navies was a case of failed "minimum deterrence." The battle might have been avoided had the Athenians sent a much larger fleet to intimidate the Corinthians; Kagan, *On the Origins of War and the Preservation of Peace* (New York: Anchor Books, 1995), pp. 45–48. Maybe so. Maybe Athens could have avoided war at that time had Pericles communicated his intentions with a bigger show of force, but in many ways Kagan's approach puts the cart before the horse. It stresses the mechanics of how the war started at the expense of the motives

of the belligerents. It focuses on strategic miscalculation, which is important, but not as important for Thucydides as the incompatible objectives of the belligerents. Without the clashing objectives, there would have been no war—which is why Thucydides treats them as the truest causes.

15. Of the speeches in his account Thucydides said, "Some I heard myself, others I got from various quarters; it was in all cases difficult to carry them word for word in one's memory, so my practice has been to make the speakers say what was demanded of them by the various occasions, of course adhering as closely as possible to the general sense of what they actually said" (1.22). No doubt, there is a possible tension between what Thucydides thought the occasion demanded and what was actually said, though he indicates he followed what was actually said as much as possible. Proof that he adhered to this principle is that sometimes the speakers say things that contradict their persuasive purposes—that is, were not what Thucydides believed their situations demanded. At other times, they say much more than is required by their rhetorical objectives, raising the question whether they are actually saying something that helps us understand them better or Thucydides used the occasion of their speeches to promote reflection on more universal, even philosophical, subjects, or both. Surely one reason for the work being a possession for all time is that it was meant to present, and generally succeeds in presenting, a microcosm of all war. The forensic character of the debates often supplies something like a dialectical approach, giving readers opportunities to see multiple sides of a question. Like citizens in Athens and Sparta, readers get to decide for themselves. See Kagan, *Outbreak of the Peloponnesian War*, p. ix; and F. E. Adcock, *Thucydides and His History* (Cambridge, U.K.: Cambridge Univ. Press, 1963), pp. 27–42.

16. Donald Kagan makes much of the "hawk and dove" split in *Outbreak of the Peloponnesian War*, pp. 77, 268, 291. Paul Rahe, "The Peace of Nicias," in *The Making of Peace: Rulers, States, and the Aftermath of War*, ed. Williamson Murray and Jim Lacey (Cambridge, U.K.: Cambridge Univ. Press, 2009), pp. 1–69, acknowledges the split, but in a brilliant critique of Kagan, his former teacher,

he more accurately places Pericles in the camp of the Athenian hawks, the followers of Themistocles, rather than the doves, the followers of Cimon.

17. Clausewitz, *On War*, p. 69.

18. Platias and Koliopoulos, *Thucydides on Strategy*, pp. 4–7.

19. See, for example, Donald Kagan, *The Archidamean War* (Ithaca, N.Y.: Cornell Univ. Press, 1975), pp. 17–42; Platias and Koliopoulos, *Thucydides on Strategy*, pp. 35–60; Connor, *Thucydides*, p. 54; Cawkwell, *Thucydides and the Peloponnesian War*, p. 43; and Hanson, *War like No Other*, p. 20.

20. An exception to the rule is Paul Rahe, who shows the extent to which Athenian diplomacy under Pericles was directed at detaching Corinth from the Peloponnesian League, with the dismemberment of the Peloponnesian League a prelude to Athenian expansion after Sparta had been defeated. Rahe, "Peace of Nicias," pp. 50, 58, 61.

21. Tritle, *New History of the Peloponnesian War*, p. 39.

22. Clausewitz, *On War*, pp. 77, 97, 137, 184–88. For Clausewitz, these moral factors are not limited to belief in the justice of one's cause or the legitimacy of the means by which one fights, though these are vital. The moral factors include all the intangibles (leadership, training, discipline, will, patriotism, enthusiasm, strategy, etc.) that make a difference, especially for morale, but that cannot be counted when belligerents go to war.

23. See the National Commission on Terrorist Attacks upon the United States, *9/11 Commission Report: Final Report of the National Commission on Terrorist Attacks upon the United States* (New York: W. W. Norton, 2004), pp. 339–48.

24. Clausewitz, *On War*, p. 88.

25. For an insightful discussion of the passion for honor and contests for rank in this war, see J. E. Lendon, *Song of Wrath: The Peloponnesian War Begins* (New York: Basic Books, 2010), but beware leaping from the frying pan of one form of reductionism (modern realism) into another (understanding everything in the Peloponnesian War in terms of honor and revenge). Said the Athenian envoys in Sparta,

they were driven to acquire, sustain, and expand their empire by three of the strongest passions in human nature—fear, honor, and interest (the desire for gain) (1.75–76). Modern realists, lacking Lendon's understanding of Greek culture and society, often underrate the role of honor in the origins, conduct, and termination of this war, but Thucydidean realism embraces the whole of human nature, not just one part, like the love of honor. If one focuses on honor exclusively, the result will still be a caricature, just a different one than common today. And while it is valuable to understand that the belligerents were not always, or even often, the "rational actors" of modern realist theory, it is misleading to make them simply irrational actors in a protracted Homeric saga of rank and revenge, as if they had no strategic vision beyond paying back their adversaries. Like humanity itself, they were a mixture of both reason and unreason, and thus capable of both serious strategic thinking and monumental strategic errors. Like Clausewitz, Thucydides deliberately eschewed monocausal explanations. His "trinity" of fear, honor, and interest is fundamentally more balanced than the templates commonly applied to his work, and it helps us evaluate the strategic rationality of the belligerents, especially when they get carried away with some great passion. That trinity serves as the launching pad, not the conclusion, of his investigation of human nature, which was perhaps his fundamental purpose. That investigation was the ultimate ground of his primary thesis—that all wars will be like the Peloponnesian War, so long as human nature remains the same (1.22), though different wars will express and reveal different aspects of human nature according to their particular circumstances.

26. Machiavelli perhaps best explained why it was utopian for *any* Greek city to seek the universal dominion later acquired by Rome. For the Greeks, citizenship was a prize and therefore restricted to a few; conquered peoples were usually not allowed to become citizens. So the more a Greek city expanded the weaker it would become, as it ran out of citizens for occupation and colonization and its subjects began to rebel. In contrast, Rome extended citizenship to those it found useful among conquered peoples, thus enabling it to expand territorially and grow stronger militarily. As Edward Gibbon, Machiavelli's student in this regard, observed, however, this more inclusive way of running an empire, which allowed assimilation of foreign cults and religions, including Christianity, may have undermined some of the spirit required to maintain the empire. See Niccolò Machiavelli, *Discourses on Livy,* trans. Harvey C. Mansfield, Jr., and Nathan Tarcov (Chicago: Univ. of Chicago Press, 1996), p. 22; and Edward Gibbon, *The History of the Decline and Fall of the Roman Empire* (London: Penguin, 1994), vol. 1, chap. 15, pp. 446–512.

27. Abraham Lincoln, "Address before the Young Men's Lyceum of Springfield, Illinois" (1838), in *The Collected Works of Abraham Lincoln,* ed. Roy P. Basler (New Brunswick, N.J.: Rutgers Univ. Press, 1953).

28. Clausewitz, *On War,* p. 585; see also Sun Tzu, *Art of War,* p. 74.

29. See Donald Kagan, *The Fall of the Athenian Empire* (Ithaca, N.Y.: Cornell Univ., 1987), p. 399.

30. Sun Tzu, *Art of War,* p. 131.

31. For a characteristically brilliant discussion of this and other associated problems of war termination, see Michael I. Handel, *Masters of War: Classical Strategic Thought* (London: Routledge, 2005), pp. 195–214.

32. See, for example, Thucydides's discussion of the first Spartan religious pretext for going to war and the Athenians' no less twisted religious counterdemand, at 1.126–138.

33. For a discussion of *hubris* and *nemesis* in Thucydides, see, of course, F. M. Cornford, *Thucydides Mythistoricus* (London: Routledge, 1907), and Christopher Coker, *Barbarous Philosophers: Reflections on the Nature of War from Heraclitus to Heisenberg* (London: Hurst, 2010), pp. 63–76. Cornford suggests Thucydides imposed the tragic art form on his history, but the history of states balancing against those seeking hegemony suggests something more like a natural law, an action/reaction phenomenon rooted in anarchic systems more analogous in this case to the theory developed by Kenneth Waltz, *Theory of International Politics* (New York: Random House, 1979), pp. 102–28. For an insightful realist critique of Athenian imperialism for failing, among other things, to respect this natural system of checks and balances, see

Lowell S. Gustafson, "Thucydides and Pluralism," in *Thucydides' Theory of International Relations: A Lasting Possession,* ed. Lowell S. Gustafson (Baton Rouge: Louisiana State Univ. Press, 2000), pp. 174–94.

34. For a thorough discussion of Alcibiades and ambition, see Steven Forde, *The Ambition to Rule: Alcibiades and the Politics of Imperialism in Thucydides* (Ithaca, N.Y.: Cornell Univ. Press, 1989).

35. Kagan, *Fall of the Athenian Empire,* pp. 325–79; Xenophon, *Hellenika,* ed. Robert B. Strassler (New York: Pantheon, 2009), 1.6.29–2.23.

36. For insightful discussions of Korea as a cradle of conflict analogous to the Peloponnesian War, see David R. McCann and Barry S. Strauss, eds., *War and Democracy: A Comparative Study of the Korean War and the Peloponnesian War* (London: M. E. Sharpe, 2001).